BIRD NEST FINDER

Identifying Aboveground Bird Nests in Eastern North America

written and illustrated by
DORCAS S. MILLER

Nature Study
Guild Publishers
an imprint of AdventureKEEN

T0191127

START HERE

Nests can be tiny to huge, ephemeral to long-lasting, a clutch of twigs or an elaborate, beautifully crafted home. With patience and time, you can learn about the secret lives of birds, who source local materials and use only their bill and toes to build. Here's how to begin:

Coverage area

1. Review the next seven pages so you know the basic terms and materials.

2. Go to the Entry Key on p. 9. Which option best describes your nest?

3. Proceed to the section key, review the possibilities, and make your choice.

There are always puzzles. You may be able to identify to group but not genus, genus but not species. Maybe the nest does not fit any category—so perplexing! Remember that important features may be missing because the nest was abandoned in progress, it's an unfinished "decoy" (p. 8), or other birds or mammals have raided the nest for building materials. This pocket-size guide features common (and a few uncommon but charismatic) birds, but there are many more species in the book's range.

When to explore? Only approach if the adult or adults have abandoned the nest, or after the chicks have fledged and departed. **Then you may look at and touch empty nests, but you may not take them.**

Bird nests are protected under the Migratory Bird Treaty Act (1916), and federal law prohibits their possession without a permit from the U.S. Fish and Wildlife Service.

© 2024 Dorcas S. Miller (text and illustrations) • ISBN 978-0-912550-42-8 • Printed in China • Cataloging-in-Publication data is available from the Library of Congress • naturestudy.com

TIPS FOR FINDING NESTS

Nest finding is a learned skill; the more you practice, the better you become.

- Instead of *looking for a nest*, scan broadly—including treetops—letting your eyes rest on anything that seems different.

- Autumn, just after leaf drop, is the prime time because nests lose their camouflage and are much more visible. Also, weather degrades nests, so important features may be lost.

- Start with productive areas such as thickets, borders of roads, and easily accessible stream and pond edges.

- In winter, check for snow cones—nests with a distinctive dollop on top.

- Eyes are better than binoculars when scanning, but binoculars are helpful for details.

- Beware of decoys: A fist-size growth of lichen perched on a limb (left) may look like a nest, and a mass dangling from a branch may be an old tent caterpillar cocoon (flattish, disheveled); a Northern Parula nest (in a clump of lichen); or a three-dimensional, carefully constructed bird nest.

- An accumulation of sticks high in a tree may be the nest of a hawk, eagle, heron, osprey—or, with the addition of exterior leaves, the nest of a squirrel.

TO IDENTIFY A NEST

Some nests are easy. A Baltimore Oriole weaves a silvery pouch that hangs from the branch of a deciduous tree. Vireos construct a stiff, basketlike cup in the fork of a horizontal limb. An Eastern Phoebe nests on a building or under a bridge or other structure, using mud, grasses, and a layer of moss on the outside. For other birds, you need more information.

What's the habitat? Along a woodland edge? In brushy pasture, old farmland, cut or burned woodlands? Along borders of ponds, streams, or wooded swamps? Near human habitation? Most of the section keys provide habitat information. It's tempting to focus on the nest itself, but habitat is the first point of reference. Birds build their nests in preferred areas, so this information can help you eliminate some species and more carefully consider others.

What supports the nest? A shrub, sapling, or tree—and is it coniferous or deciduous? A building or other structure? Is it in a tree cavity or tunneled into a bank of gravel, sand, or earth?

Where is the nest? On a horizontal branch? Out on a limb or next to the trunk? In the crotch of a shrub, sapling, or tree? In a thicket, supported by many small branches or vines? And how far from the ground?

What materials do you see? Some birds use grass, grass, and more grass. Others use twigs, sticks, or branches. Grapevine bark may be a prominent feature. Does the nest have a thick layer of downy material as the lining? Is the exterior garnished with birch bark curls or pieces of light-green lichen? Each of these observations is significant. See the following pages for a visual glossary of materials; this glossary will be particularly helpful when deciding whether the nest contains rootlets or roots, twiglets or small twigs, large twigs or sticks, and so on.

WHAT SHAPE IS THE NEST?

Saucer: Much wider than deep

Cup saddled on limb (saddled on horizontal fork, p. 34; saddled on branch with uprights, p. 33)

Basketlike cup hanging from fork or limb

Cup built in crotch or upright fork

Platform: Small, if any, indentation

Various strategies birds use to hold the nest together

Weave flexible materials.

Strategically place woody twigs and sticks.

Fasten the nest to uprights.

Place the nest in a cavity or other container, or a crotch that provides strength and protection.

Use mud as a matrix to glue the other materials together.

Stretch sticky, elastic spider orb silk or caterpillar strands around the exterior.

Plaster pieces of paper from a paper wasp nest on the exterior.

Note: The Chimney Swift is the only bird in this book that uses saliva to glue sticks together and glue the nest to the wall.

ROOTS, BARK, TWIGS, STICKS, AND OTHER MATERIALS

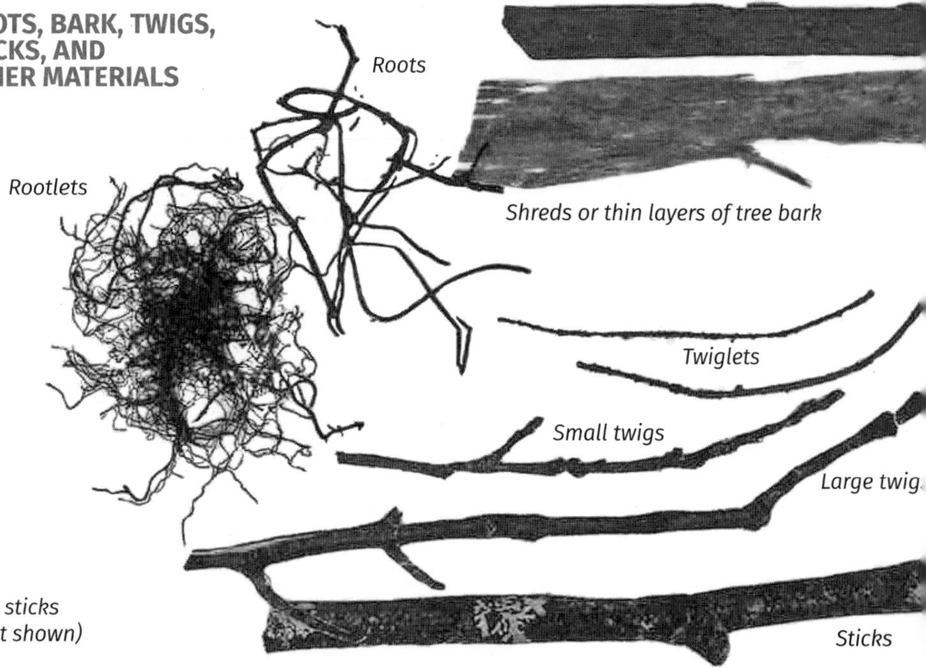

Roots

Rootlets

Shreds or thin layers of tree bark

Twiglets

Small twigs

Large twig

Big sticks
(not shown)

Sticks

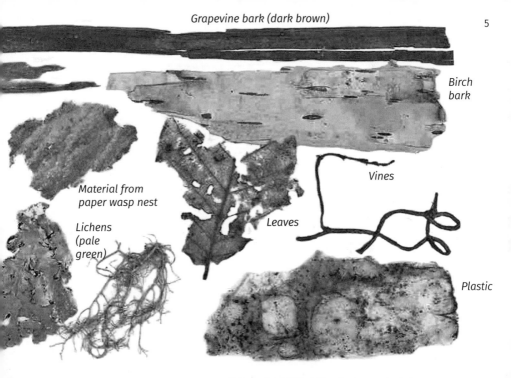

Grapevine bark (dark brown)

Birch bark

Material from paper wasp nest

Lichens (pale green)

Leaves

Vines

Plastic

GRASSES, STEMS, FIBERS, AND FLUFF

Fine grasses

Grass leaves

Plant stems (nonwoody "weed" stems)

Twine

Sticky orb strands from spiderweb (not shown)

Tarp fibers

Fibers from outer layer of milkweed stem

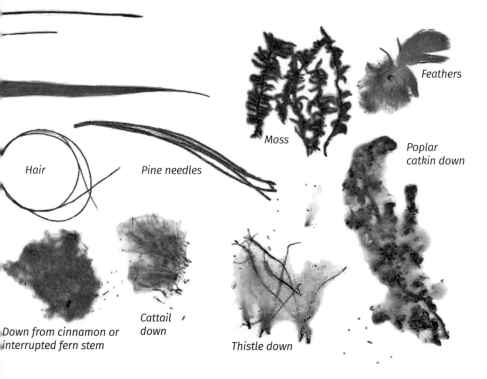

Feathers

Moss

Poplar
catkin down

Hair

Pine needles

Down from cinnamon or
interrupted fern stem

Cattail
down

Thistle down

ABBREVIATIONS AND OTHER USEFUL INFORMATION

Numbers: Nest diameter and nest height are measurements of the outside of the nest. Nest diameter 4" [–10"]: The average diameter is 4", but a nest can be as large as 10".

Abbreviations: D = Nest diameter   H = Nest height   G = Aboveground   ~ = Approximately

Names: In ornithology, the style is to capitalize the first letter of common names but leave that letter lowercase when referring to more than one species: Rose-breasted Grosbeak vs. grosbeaks.

Look, photograph, sketch, take notes, and leave nests in place. Why? End-of-season nests are a source of building materials for both birds and mammals. Many birds (including swallows, orioles, cuckoos, Blue Jays, grosbeaks, ospreys, Mourning Doves, and some raptors, herons, and egrets) sometimes or regularly reuse their nests. Taking nests is against the law.

Extra, partly built nests: Some species* build more than one nest. The extras may provide decoys to protect the actual site, serve as backup homes in case the first nest is destroyed, or showcase the male's prowess.
Bluebirds, chickadees, crows, kingfishers, Tree Swallows, wrens, some woodpeckers

Do chicks poop in the nest? When birds feed their chicks, the young immediately produce a fecal sac, which the parent snatches away and eats—it still contains nutrition—or removes from the site to keep the nest sanitary and prevent odors that might attract predators. Just before fledging, young of some species, such as goldfinches, grackles, and martins, leave feces in the nest or on the rim; rain may carry the white uric acid in the feces down the outside, making the nest whitish.

Shortcuts: *Saucer or platform?* Mourning Doves, cuckoos, Blue Jays, grosbeaks, many herons, and egrets. *In a colony?* Grackles, Purple Martins, Cliff and sometimes Barn Swallows, many herons, and egrets.

ENTRY KEY Page

* Thicket: Dense vegetation such as a tangle of vines, briers, canes, woody vegetation; includes dense stands of cedar or other conifers, as well as thick shrubbery along roads and in hedgerows. Thickets are so common that they have been placed in their own key.

in.   1   2   3   4   5

NEST HANGS FROM TWIG OR IS TIED TO UPRIGHTS

	D	H	G	Notes	Exterior garnished	Page
A. WOODLANDS	Orioles build a pouch; vireos build a basketlike cup.					
● *In tree (RE Vireo, BH Vireo also in shrub), away from trunk, hanging from forked twig*						
Oriole, Orchard	3.5–4"	5" [3.5–8"]	10–20' [–70']	Long green grasses that dry yellow		11
Baltimore	3"	5" [3.5–8"]	20–30' [6–60']	Silvery fibers and other materials		11
Vireo, Red-eyed	2.75–3"	2.5"	5–15'	In hardwood	Yes	13
Yellow-throated	3"	2.5–3"	20–50'	In hardwood	Yes	13
Warbling	3.25" at widest	2–3"	20–50+'	In hardwood	No	13
Blue-headed	3–3.5"	2.5–3.5"	3–20'	Usually in conifer	Yes	13
● *In mass of* Usnea *lichen, Spanish moss, etc., from a branch; may bulge like oriole*						
Northern Parula	~3"	—	10–40'	In hardwood or conifer		12
B. WETLANDS	Cup bound to reeds, cattails, rushes; blackbird, Yellowthroat sometimes in low shrub					
Blackbird, Red-winged	4–7"	3–7"	4–17'	May be loosely colonial		15
Wren, Marsh	5"	7"	2–6'	Nest covered, side entrance		15
Common Yellowthroat	3–3.5"	3"	Inches–3'	Also in thickets, shrubby fields		14

in. | 1 | 2 | 3 | 4 | 5

BALTIMORE ORIOLE

Often a bag of silvery fibers; visible in early spring, fall— before and after leaves

WHERE: Open woodlands; along roads; in parks, orchards, or suburbs

BUILDER AND MATERIALS: The female pulls fibrous strings from stems of milkweed or dogbane, strips from grapevines, and other materials. She collects fine materials for the lining.

D: 3–4"   H: 5" [3.5–8"]   G: 20–30'   Opening: 2–3"

The pouch stretches as the chicks grow, becoming spherical or gourd-shaped.

ORCHARD ORIOLE

Rather than fibers, *female uses long green grass blades that dry yellowish tan.*

WHERE: Open woodlands, often along wetlands, ponds, rivers; also in shade trees (for example, elms before they were decimated by Dutch elm disease)

D: ~4"   H: ~3"   G: 10–20'

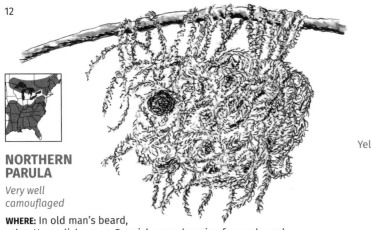

Red-eyed
Vireo

Yellow-throated
Vireo

Warbling
Vireo

Blue-headed
Vireo

NORTHERN PARULA

Very well camouflaged

WHERE: In old man's beard,
other *Usnea* lichens, or Spanish moss hanging from a branch;
if these are not available, in clumped twigs; in mixed or
coniferous woodlands

BUILDER AND MATERIALS: The female creates a cavity in the hanging
mass, then adds some soft material as lining.

Cup inside cavity
D: 3"   H: 2"   G: 10–40' [–100']

in.   1   2   3   4   5

VIREOS

	Red-eyed	Yellow-throated	Warbling	Blue-headed
HABITAT:	Deciduous or mixed with understory	Open deciduous or mixed; along borders or in open areas	Mature deciduous; often borders water	Coniferous or mixed woodlands
MATERIALS:	Grapevine bark, birch bark, other materials	Strips of inner bark, dry grass, rootlets	Shreds (not strips) of inner bark	Bark strips, grasses, plant fibers, down
D:	2.75–3"	2.5–3"	3–3.5"	2.5–3.5"
G:	To 20'	Greater than 20'	25–50' [2–90']	To 20'
GARNISHED:	Wasp nest paper, birch bark strips	Lichen dots, moss, cocoons, leaves	None	Bark curls

ALL SPECIES: Use fine grasses, other soft materials for lining; spiderweb silk holds exterior materials in place.

All nest in hardwood except Blue-headed.

RE, BH nest to 20' from the ground; YT, warbling nest 20+'.

Red-eyed Vireo nest

D: 3–3.5"
H: 3"
G: To 3'

COMMON YELLOWTHROAT

Roundish cup; thick felting; often near water

WHERE: In cattails, low shrub, or tree; usually next to salt or fresh wetlands; also in upland areas with thickets, scrubby fields, dense shrubs

BUILDER AND MATERIALS: Female weaves a bulky cup of reeds, coarse grass, and plant stems, tying the cup to adjacent uprights; she lines it with fine grasses.

MARSH WREN

Globe- or football-shaped, near water

WHERE: In marshes, cattails, reeds, low shrubs

BUILDER AND MATERIALS: Male, using reeds, coarse grass, plant stems; female lines with grasses, rootlets, and down.

D: 5"
H: 7"
G: 2–6'

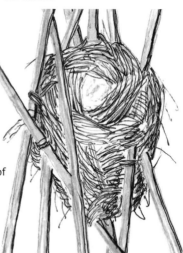

RED-WINGED BLACKBIRD

Open marsh; tied to reeds or in crotch

WHERE: Often in cattails or upland clover fields

BUILDER AND MATERIALS: The female builds a rough structure (sometimes over water) using coarse grass, then packs gaps with bits of wood, plant down, lichen, moss, and, on occasion, mud.

D: 4–7"   H: 3–7"   G: 4–17'

RW and YH Blackbirds may loosely congregate by species or with each other.

YELLOW-HEADED BLACKBIRD

Similar to RW nest (borders marsh, made of grasses, in colonies) but near ground and always over water

RANGE: WI, most of MN and IA, northern IL

D: 5–6"   H: 5–6"   G: 2–4'

in.   1   2   3   4   5

NEST 1–3.5" DIAMETER, CUP-SHAPED S = SADDLED, C = CROTCH

	D	H	G	Features	Page
A. LINING THICKLY FELTED with down from poplar catkins, ferns, cattails, thistles, similar fluff					
Hummingbird	1–2.25"	1–1.25"	10–40'	S Tiny; in deciduous tree or conifer; exterior dotted with bits of lichen	18
Warbler, Yellow	3"	2.5"	3–10' [–40']	C Thick walled; no droppings	18
Goldfinch, Am.	3"	2" [–4.5"]	4–14' [–20']	C Thick walled; late in season droppings in nest, around rim; whitewash on exterior	19
Flycatcher, Least	2.4–3"	2 [1.6–2.6"]	2–15' [–60']	C or S Thin walled; no droppings	M 17
B. LINING NOT THICKLY FELTED but may include moss, rootlets, hair, feathers, fluff					
Alder Flycatcher	3.1"	2.9"	To 6'	C or S Deciduous shrub; trailing streamers; exterior untidy; lining of feathers	M 17
Wood-Pewee	3"	1–2"	15–20+'	C Deciduous tree; lichen dots on exterior	19
Warblers (So many warblers, so little space; representative low-nesting species included here.)					
BT Blue	3.5"	2.25" [–4.5"]	3–5'	C Shrub, sapling; bark curls, black rootlets	21
C-sided	2.8"	2.6"	1–3' [–6']	C Deciduous shrub; loose nest, thin walls	M 17
Prairie	3.25"	3"	3–7' [–10']	C Deciduous or coniferous shrub; contains down, hair, fur	20–21
Redstart	2.75x3"	3.25"	1–10'	C Shrub, tree; usually deciduous; compact	20
Yellowthroat	3–3.5"	3"	0.5–3'	Bound to low shrub or reeds	14
C. LINING OF FINE GRASSES AND OTHER SOFT MATERIALS			**Indigo Bunting D: 3.25–4.5"**		29

HABITAT

A.

Ruby-throated Hummingbird: Open woodland, deciduous or mixed; various open habitats (brushy fields, road edges, meadows); near human habitation; woodland edges

American Goldfinch: Brushy fields, road edges, meadows, open habitats; near human habitation

Yellow Warbler: Thickets, including roadside; along streams and wetlands

Least Flycatcher: Semi- and fully open woodlands; near human habitation

B.

Alder Flycatcher: Wet thickets, alders; dense briers, shrubs, saplings

Eastern Wood-Pewee: Open woodlands, especially clearings and edges; roadside edges; shade trees

Black-throated Blue: Thick growth in mixed hardwoods

Chestnut-sided Warbler: Dense briers, shrubs, saplings

Prairie Warbler: Shrubby areas with open woods, pastures, burns, slash, barrens

American Redstart: Wet thickets, wetlands, ponds, streams

Common Yellowthroat: Wetlands, upland areas with thickets

C.

Indigo Bunting: Thicket; open, brushy areas; edges; burns

Alder
Flycatcher

Least
Flycatcher

Chestnut-
sided Warbler

in. | 1 | 2 | 3 | 4 | 5

RUBY-THROATED HUMMINGBIRD

Hard to spot in tree; resembles a clump of lichen

WHERE: Usually on down-sloping branch

BUILDER AND MATERIALS: Female makes a base of bud scales; uses small, pinkish-tan hairs from spring ferns or other down for the cup; garnishes the exterior with tips from flat lichen. Then she binds the nest with caterpillar or spider webbing so the nest can expand as chicks grow.

D: 1–2.5"   H: 1–1.25"   G: 10–40'

YELLOW WARBLER

WHERE: *Thickets along roadsides, power line cuts; streams and wetlands,* often in alder, willow

MATERIALS: *Fine grasses, narrow bark strips; whitish fibers, patches of down, artificial batting on exterior;* lining of catkin and fern down

**D: 3"   H: 2.5"   G: 3–10' [–40']
Inner depth: 1.25–1.5"**

See Goldfinch, opposite.

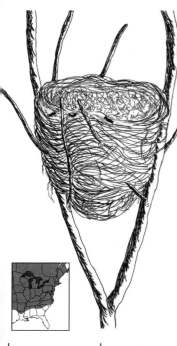

Similar to Yellow Warbler: Consider habitat, exterior materials, and number of uprights (goldfinch has 3 or more).

AMERICAN GOLDFINCH

HABITAT: *Overgrown fields, open country*

MATERIALS: *Fine grasses*, perhaps with bark strips, rootlets, moss; *lining thistle down* or other fluff; *may have whitewash or droppings on upper exterior (p. 8), but no wads of down or artificial batting; sometimes wider than high*

D: 3"   H: 2.75–3" [–4.5"]   G: 4–1' [–20']   Inner depth: 1.6"

EASTERN WOOD-PEWEE

From below, resembles clump of rag lichen (p. 1)

Often on horizontal branch away from trunk; lichen on outside like hummingbird, but nest made of twigs, grass, roots (not plant down)

D: 3"   H: 1–2"   G: 15–20+'

in.   1   2   3   4   5

AMERICAN REDSTART

Compact, tightly woven; crotch

WHERE: Near water (wetlands, alder or willow thickets), fields, or second-growth woodlands with thick shrubs

BUILDER AND MATERIALS: Female builds with narrow bark strips and grass blades, fine rootlets, weed stems, grasses, and twiglets, along with plant down, feathers, moss, pine needles, lichens, and other materials. Down may be used in patches throughout. Feathers, lichen, and bits of birch bark may dot the exterior.

D: 2.75–3"   H: 3.25"   G: 1–10'   Inner depth: 1.5"

PRAIRIE WARBLER (right)

For lining, plant down, fur, feathers

WHERE: Thick, low understory in mature woodlands; also in low shrubs in burns, power cuts, former fields, cut-over areas; despite name, not found on open prairie

BUILDER AND MATERIALS: Female uses bark shreds, fine grasses, soft plant fibers such as fern pubescence, and down, then lines with hair, feathers, and more grasses.

D: 3"   H: 3"   G: 3–7'   Inner depth: 2"

BLACK-THROATED BLUE WARBLER

Often birch bark curls on exterior, black rootlets in lining

WHERE: Understory; rhododendron, viburnum, other impenetrable shrubs; also small trees such as balsam fir

BUILDER AND MATERIALS: Female uses thin bark strips, grasses, and twigs. She lines with fine rootlets, rootlets, and/or black horsehair lichen, then decorates the exterior with birch bark. Spider webbing holds everything in place.

D: 3.5" **H:** 2.25" [–4.5"] **G:** 3–5' **Inner depth:** 1.5"

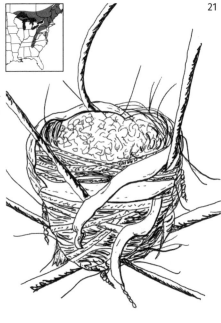

SUMMARY 4–10" NESTS

IN A THICKET (P. 9)		NOT IN A THICKET		
May be saddled or in a crotch	D	Saddled on a branch	Tucked in a crotch	G
Bunting, Indigo (p. 29)	3.25–4.5"		Bunting, Indigo	To 3'
Cardinal, Northern (p. 38)	4"			4' [–10']
Catbird, Gray (p. 39)	5.5–6"			3' [–10']
Chat, Yellow-breasted (p. 32)	5–6"			1–8'
Cuckoo, BB (p. 40)	8"	(Also saddled in dense vegetation)		7' [–20']
Cuckoo, YB (p. 40)	5–6"	(Also saddled in dense vegetation)		4–20' [–90']
	8"	Dove, Mourning (p. 41)	Dove, Mourning	10–25' [–50']
	7"	Finch, Purple (p. 28)		5–20' [–60']
	6–9"	Grackle, Common (p. 35)		To 60'
Grosbeak, RB (p. 37)	3.5–9"		Grosbeak, RB	3–8' [–30']
Grosbeak, Blue (p. 37)	~4.5–5"		Grosbeak, Blue	3–10'
	7–8"	Jay, Blue (p. 43)	Jay, Blue	10–25'
	5.5–7"	Kingbird, Eastern (p. 33)	Kingbird	~10–20'
Mockingbird (p. 42)	7"	Mockingbird		3–10' [–20']
	6–8"	Robin, American (p. 34)		5–25'
Sparrow, Chipping (p. 30)	4.5"	Sparrow, Chipping		4–10'
Sparrow, Field (p. 28, 30)	4–5"	Sparrow, Field		1–10'
Sparrow, Song (p. 28, 30)	4–9"			Inches–15'
	12"	Thrasher, Brown (p. 36)		2–7" [–14"]
	4–6"	Thrush, Wood (M p. 34)	Thrush, Wood	5–50'
	4–5.5"	Waxwing, Cedar (p. 31)	Waxwing	3–20' [–50']

NEST 4–10" IN THICKET OR TANGLE OF VINES, BRIERS; IN DENSE SHRUBS OR A BRUSH PILE; IN A THICK STAND OF YOUNG CONIFERS Habitat info (p. 28)

Waxwing (p. 31) usually saddled or in crotch of shrub or tree; may also be in dense conifers.

	D	H	G	Features	Page
A. CHIEFLY OF GRASSES; SOMEWHAT OR VERY THICK WALLED					
Bunting, Indigo	3.25–4.5"	2.5–3"	Low–3'	In a crotch	29
Chat, YB	5–6"	3"	1–8'	Saddled, bulky, sprawling	32
Sparrow, Field	4–5"	2.5"	1–10'	Saddled, bulky; in hardwood	28, 30
Chipping	4–5"	2.3"	4–10'	Saddled; favors conifer but uses either	30
Song	4–9"	2.5–4.5"	Inches–15'	Saddled; larger than Chipping, Field	28, 30
B. CHIEFLY OF TWIGS, BARK STRIPS, OTHER MATERIALS; SOME SPECIES INCLUDE STICKS, GRASSES					
Platform or saucer on horizontal branch or fork					
Cuckoo, BB	8"	~1"	7' [–20']	Better built; lining thicker	M 40
Cuckoo, YB	5–6"	1.5"	4–90'	Twigs loose; lining thin	40
Cup (RB Grosbeak shallow)					
Cardinal	~4"	2–3"	3–15'	Rough, not sprawling; sometimes has trash	38
Catbird, Gray	5.5–6"	3"	3' [–10']	Loosely built, straggling; often has trash	39
Grosbeak, Blue	~4.5–5"	—	3–10'	Compact; inner cup 2–3" deep	37
Grosbeak, RB	3.5–9"	1.5–5"	3–8' [–30']	Very loose; inner cup 3–6" deep	37
Mockingbird	7"	4.5"	3–10' [–20']	Sprawling; often contains trash	42

NEST 4–10" SADDLED ON A BRANCH; MAY BE NESTLED BETWEEN UPRIGHTS

	D	H	G	Features	Page
A. MOSTLY GRASSES AND GRASS STEMS, WITHOUT MUD					
Finch, Purple	7"	4"	4–60'	Shrub, tree; away from trunk; loosely built	M 28
Kingbird	5.5–7"	2–3.25"	10–20'	Shrub or low tree; often in exposed location	33
Sparrow, Chipping	4–5"	2.3"	4–10'	Favors conifers but uses either; near humans	30
Sparrow, Field	4–5"	2.5"	1–10'	Low shrub; bulky, thick walled	28, 30
Waxwing, Cedar	4–5.5"	3–4"	3–20' [–50']	Bulky; thick walled	31
B. PLANT STEMS WITH MUD AS BASE OR INNER SHELL					
(mud occasional for blackbird, p. 15; grackle, below)					
Grackle	6–9"	4–8"	To 60'	Shrub or tree, mud occasional	35
Phoebe, Eastern	4–4.5"	2–4"	—	usually on building, but can nest in the wild	57
Robin, American	6–8"	3–6"	5–25'	Tree; interior shell of mud; lined with grasses	34
Thrush, Wood	4–6"	2–5.75"	5–50'	Shrub, sapling; mud shell; lined with rootlets	34
C. TWIGS AND SMALL STEMS					
Dove, Mourning	8"	Flat	10–25' [–50']	Tree; minimal nest, thin platform layer	41
Jay (saucer)	7–8"	4–4.5"	10–25'	Next to trunk or out on horizontal limb	43
Mockingbird	7"	4.5"	3–10' [–20']	Sprawling; base twigs; often with trash	42
Thrasher	12"	3.75"	2–7' [–14']	Tidy; sticks to 1' long, sometimes thorny	36
D. STICKS; NEST A PLATFORM OR SAUCER (also Mourning Dove, above)					
Cuckoo, BB	8"	~1"	7' [–20']	Better built; lining thicker	M 40
Cuckoo, YB	5–6"	~1.5"	4–90'	Twigs loose; lining thin	40
Heron, Green	8–12"	—	~10–33'	Colonial nester	45

HABITAT

A. **Finch, Purple:** Wooded areas (conifer, mixed, suburbs with shade trees; sometimes along streams); near human habitation

Kingbird, Eastern: Road, woodland edges; brushy fields, other open habitats; often over water

Sparrow, Chipping: Woodlands (grassy openings, edges); near trees along roadsides, parks, shady backyards; often on branch of small conifer.

Sparrow, Field: Road or woodland edges, brushy fields, other open habitats

Waxwing, Cedar: Open deciduous, coniferous, and mixed woods; often along streams, rivers

B. **Grackle, Common:** Urban, suburban, and agricultural areas; pine plantations in the South; open woodlands and edges; wetlands and along wooded streams; meadows

Phoebe, Eastern: In the wild, in steep, rocky, protected area; on buildings, under bridges

Robin, American: Open woods, open areas near human habitation (fields, parks, lawns, etc.)

Thrush, Wood: Mature forest with some understory and open ground and water nearby

C. **Dove, Mourning:** Open woods, roadsides, near human habitation

Jay, Blue: Woodlands and edges; near human habitation

Mockingbird, Northern: Road edges, brushy fields, other open habitats

Thrasher, Brown: Road and woodland edges, brushy fields, other open habitats

D. **Cuckoo, Black-billed:** Thickets or dense shrubbery in wet openings in deciduous woods

Cuckoo, Yellow-billed: Thickets or dense shrubs, trees (deciduous or coniferous) in woodland, field, near stream or road edges

Heron, Green: Thicket, shrub, or tree near or over water

NEST 4–10" LOCATED IN CROTCH (Cuckoos, p. 40, may build in quasi-crotch)

	D	H	G	Features	Page
A. PLATFORM OR SAUCER; LOOSELY BUILT WITH THIN LAYER OF TWIGS OR STICKS OR TREE					
Dove, Mourning	8"	Flat	10–25' [–50']	In large shrub, tree; little or no lining	41
B. CUP					
Mostly grasses					
Blackbird, RW	4–7"	3–7"	4–17'	Bound to reeds but nestled in shrub	15
Bunting, Indigo	3.25–4.5"	2.5–3"	To 3'	Shrub; nest bound to uprights	29
Thrush, Wood	4–6"	2–5.75"	5–50'	Shrub, tree; mud forms interior shell	34
Waxwing, Cedar	4–5.5"	3–4"	3–20' [–50']	Bulky; prefers dense conifers	31
Variety of building materials or (jay and kingbird) chiefly woody					
Grosbeak, Blue	~4.5–5"	—	3–10'	Compact; shrub, tree, vine; often contains trash; lining rootlets, grasses	37
Grosbeak, RB	3.5–9"	1.5–5"	3–18' [–30']	Very loose; sapling, often deciduous; lining rootlets, grass; twigs often forked	37
Jay, Blue	7–8"	4–4.5"	10–25'	Often next to tree trunk; lining rootlets	43
Kingbird	5.5–7"	2–3.25"	10–20'	Shrub or low tree; often over water or other exposed location; lining grasses	33

HABITAT

A.

Dove, Mourning: In thicket, woodland edges; near human habitation

B.

Mostly Grasses

Blackbird, Red-winged: Alders, edge of wetlands in cattails, low-lying ground

Bunting, Indigo: Shrubby fields, road and woodland edges, multiflora hedges

Thrush, Wood: Cool, damp woodlands; near stream, pond

Waxwing, Cedar: Near stream, pond

Variety or woody

Grosbeak, Blue: Thickets, brambles, brushy areas

Grosbeak, Rose-breasted: Open, second woodlands, road edges, thickets; near stream, pond; shrubby fields

Jay, Blue: Near stream, pond; woodland edges; near human habitation

Kingbird, Eastern: Near stream, pond; shrubby fields; woodland edges

THICKET HABITAT (continued from p. 23)

Thickets may be found along woodland edges and roads, borders of ponds and streams, in brushy fields and pastures, old farmland, and cut or burned woodlands. Some species that nest in a thicket may also build on a branch or in a crotch in a shrub or tree, so these species are found in more than one key. (For an overview, refer to p. 22.) **Cardinals, Catbirds, Blue** and **Rose-breasted Grosbeaks, Mockingbirds,** and **Song** and **Chipping Sparrows** nest near humans.

SPARROWS (p. 30)

PURPLE FINCH (p. 24–25)

WHERE: Chiefly in cool conifer forests but also mixed forests, shady streams, and suburbs

BUILDER AND MATERIALS: Female builds on a horizontal limb away from the trunk, in a conifer in the North and a deciduous tree in the southern part of its range. She makes a twig base; uses coarse grasses, rootlets, plant stems, and strips of bark for the cup and lines with fine grasses, rootlets, hair, and/or fern down.

D: 7"   H: 4"   G: 5–20' [–50']

Finch

Field

Song

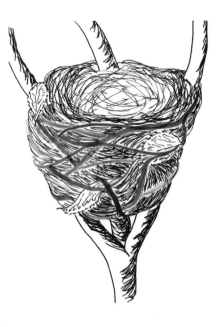

INDIGO BUNTING

Grassy nest built around uprights in crotch

WHERE: In crotch of low shrub or within thicket; open, brushy areas along roads, streams, fields, and woodland edges; burns; land harvested for timber; and other similar sites

SHAPE: May be round or oval

BUILDER AND MATERIALS: Female weaves a nest of grasses, bark strips, plant stems, dead leaves, and sometimes a few twigs; the lining consists of fine grasses and other soft materials.

D: 3.25–4.5"   H: 2.5–3"   G: Inches–3'

CHIPPING SPARROW

WHERE: Often in a conifer (pine in the Southeast, spruce in the North, juniper and evergreen ornamental shrubs wherever available)

BUILDER AND MATERIALS: Female, placing nest at tip of branch or in cradle of branches in a thicket, uses dry grass, plant stalks, and rootlets; the lining is fine grasses and hair or fur (human, horse, raccoon, deer, others).

RANGE: Throughout

	Prefers	**D**	**H**	**G**	**Found**
Chip	Conifer	4.5"	2.3"	4–10'	Saddled or in thicket near human habitation, along roadsides, openings in woodlands
Field*	Deciduous	4–5"	2.5"	1–10'	Saddled or in thicket in brushy pastures, other open areas, and along woodland edge
Song*	Either	4–9"		2.5–4.5" Inches–15'	In thicket in brushy pastures, other open areas, near human habitation

* See map p. 28

CEDAR WAXWING

Bulky, messy, thick walled; often moss or lichen on exterior

WHERE: In a crotch or saddled (sometimes between vertical twigs, shown here) on a branch in a hardwood or conifer, or in thick vines; often found along streams in open coniferous, deciduous, or mixed woodlands

BUILDER AND MATERIALS: Female does most of the work on the first nest of the season; male may help with the second. She selects from weed stems, twigs, grasses, cattail down, moss, lichens, and string, then lines with pine needles, fine grasses, and rootlets.

D: 4–5.5"   H: 3–4"   G: 3–20' [–50']

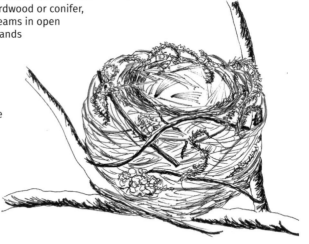

| in. | | 1 | | 2 | | 3 | | 4 | | 5 |

YELLOW-BREASTED CHAT

Bulky, sprawling, with foundation of leaves; thicket

WHERE: In a tangle of briers (often raspberry, blackberry, huckleberry, multiflora rose); vines, including grape, catbrier, honeysuckle; or sumac

BUILDER AND MATERIALS: Female lays a foundation of dead leaves and other coarse vegetation, then weaves a cup of bark strips, grasses, plant stems, and vine tendrils. Fine grasses and soft weed stems form the lining.

SIZE: This species is much larger than other wood warblers east of the Mississippi, and its nest is much larger as well.

D: 5–6" H: 3" G: 1–8'

in. | 1 | 2 | 3 | 4 | 5

EASTERN KINGBIRD

Saddled or cradled on branch; crotch

WHERE: Along banks of shrubby ponds and streams (nest may overhang water); in bushes or small trees in open woods, forest edges, fields with dispersed shrubs and trees; occasionally on stubs or stumps. Usually on horizontal branch, away from the trunk; sometimes in crotch. In either hardwood or conifer forest. Often in an exposed site (lone conifer, dead snag in bog) with a view.

SHAPE: Ragged cup; large for size of bird

BUILDER AND MATERIALS: Female uses small twigs, roots, plant stems, down, string, tarp strands, and other materials, then lines with fine grasses, down, and sometimes rootlets.

D: 5.5–7"   H: 2–3.25"   G: ~10–20'
Inner depth: 2–3"

AMERICAN ROBIN *Mud shell visible or not; exterior may be messy; saddled*

WHERE: Open woods, shade trees near fields, parks, lawns

SHAPE: Inside wall, vertical; outside, vertical or mounded profile

BUILDER AND MATERIALS: Female, after assembling a substantial base of twigs, coarse grasses, and fine grasses, shapes the structure with her breast and the wrist of her wing. She then scoops mud with her bill and applies it to the floor and walls, shaping with her body so the cup fits her nicely. The nest often includes trash. For the lining, she adds fine grasses to the still-damp mud. Areas of mud may remain visible, especially around the rim.

D: 6–8" H: 3–6" G: 5–25'

WOOD THRUSH also uses structural mud, but the nest is smaller, in a crotch or saddled, and lined with rootlets.

D: 4-6" H: 2-5.7" G: 5–50'

COMMON GRACKLE *Often in colony; grassy nest, sometimes with mud; saddled on branch*

WHERE: Regularly nests in groups, averaging 20–30 [–200]; usually high in conifer, on horizontal branch with or without uprights; also in meadows; sometimes near wetlands; in the South, in pine plantations

SHAPE: Bulky with thick walls and floor, tidy (not sprawling) cup

BUILDER AND MATERIALS: Female builds, using coarse grass, weed stalks, fine twigs; mud, paper, and string may also be included. Other materials may vary by site (e.g., seaweed near the ocean).

D: 6–9"   H: 4–8"
G: Few–60'
Inner diameter: 3.5"

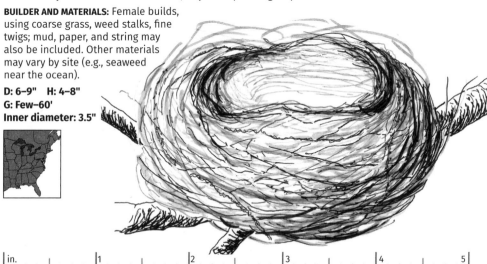

in. | 1 | 2 | 3 | 4 | 5

BROWN THRASHER

Twig platform with distinct cup; saddled

WHERE: Saddled in shrub or low tree along road or field edges; woodland borders; brushy pastures

SHAPE: Platform larger than cup; cup round with a shallow indentation

BUILDER AND MATERIALS: Both birds build a loose platform of twigs 0.1–0.2" thick and to 12" long. They layer on dead leaves, bark strips, and plant stems, then weave a cup of roots or rootlets on top. Grasses or pine needles form the lining.

Platform D: ~12"
Cup D: 4–5" [~6"]
H: 3.5"
G: 2–7' [~14']

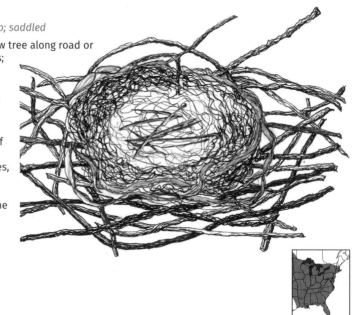

ROSE-BREASTED GROSBEAK

Loose cup, no platform; thicket; crotch

WHERE: In crotch, often in bushy deciduous sapling or shrubs; thicket in second-growth woods, road edges, wetlands; parks, near human habitation

BUILDER AND MATERIALS: On the exterior, the female, or both birds, uses twigs—some forked (to help hold the nest together?)—then weaves in coarse plant stems and fibers, narrow bark strips, and grass. The lining of rootlets, pine needles, and some grass barely fills the cracks in the loose cup/saucer.

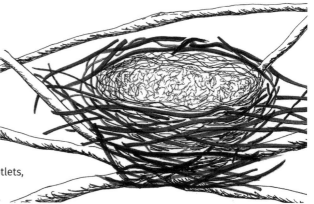

RB
D: 3.5–9"
H: 1.5–5"
G: 3–8' [–30']
Inner D: 3–6"

Blue Grosbeak
D: ~4.5–5"
H: —
G: 4–10'
Inner D: 2–3"

Uncommon; nest materials and habitats similar to RB; nest smaller, better-cupped, more compact

in. 1 2 3 4 5

NORTHERN CARDINAL

Thicket

WHERE: In deciduous or coniferous thickets along borders of woods, shrubby fields, roads, stream banks; in parks, suburbs (often in landscaping shrubs)

BUILDER AND MATERIALS: For the base, the female uses twigs that she bends and crushes to make flexible; adds a layer of leaves; then uses strips of grapevine bark, plant stems, grass, rootlets. The lining is hair and/or fine grasses.

D: 4" (twigs extend beyond)
H: 2–3" **G:** 3–15'

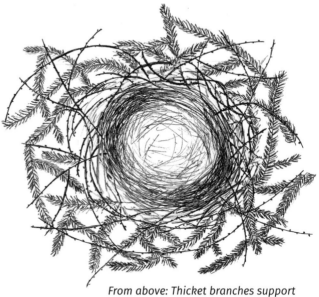

From above: Thicket branches support a loose halo of flexible twigs.

GRAY CATBIRD

Loosely built on bed of leaves; trash common; thicket

WHERE: Dense thickets in open areas such as along roads, woodland edges, and flowing water

BUILDER AND MATERIALS: Female lays down leaves that may coalesce into a layer (exposed, right), then uses long twigs, thick weed stems, grapevine bark strips, and plastic or other trash. She tucks in rootlets, grass, pine needles, and/or hair for the lining.

D: 5.5–6" H: 4" G: 3' [–10']
Inner depth: 2"

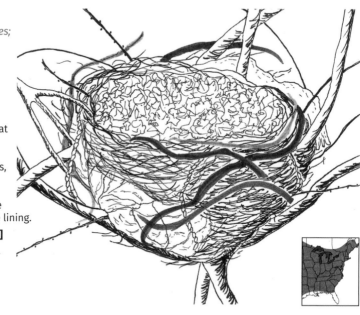

YELLOW-BILLED CUCKOO

Thicket, sometimes horizontal fork; saddled in tree/shrub

WHERE: In (usually deciduous) thicket or dense vegetation in tree or shrub; along roads, streams, wetlands; anywhere with excellent cover

BUILDER AND MATERIALS: Both birds lay down twigs and sticks, mixing in vines, rootlets, leaves, moss, and lichens. To line, they add more moss, a few pine needles, and sometimes catkins* and dried leaves. Flimsy platform/saucer of short twigs

D: 5–6" H: 1.5" G: 4–20' [–90']

Combination of large eggs (1.0x0.8") and minimal depression: Eggs easily fall from nest.

Oak catkin, left (about half size)

BLACK-BILLED CUCKOO

Larger (D 8") with thicker lining of cotton-like fibers, catkins, leaves, and pine needles

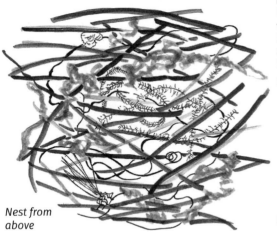

Nest from above

in. | 1 | 2 | 3 | 4 | 5

MOURNING DOVE

Flimsy platform; saddled on branch or in crotch

WHERE: Open country, including woodland edges; buildings

BUILDER AND MATERIALS: Mourning Doves are minimalist nest-builders. The male delivers twigs and perhaps a few plant stems and pine needles. The female builds a loose platform saddled on a limb; in a crotch; on top of another bird's nest from the previous year; on the flattish top of a stub; or in gutters or other flat surfaces on a building. There is no lining. The nest disintegrates in several months.

D: 8" G: 10–25' [–50']

Nest from above

NORTHERN MOCKINGBIRD

Platform; thicket; saddled on branch

WHERE: Wedged into a shrubby thicket or sprawling on a tree branch, near humans in urban and suburban parks, gardens, and similar areas; also near water and in open woodlands and edges

BUILDER AND MATERIALS: Both birds build the nest; the male starts, and the female finishes. The base is twigs, usually with string, paper, plastic, tarp strands, cloth, or other trash. Grass and rootlets line the cup.

Twigs: 7"   Cup D: 4.5"   G: 3–10' [–20']

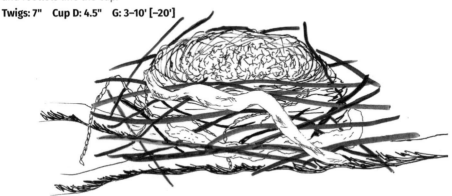

in. | 1 | 2 | 3 | 4 | 5

BLUE JAY

Viewed from below, a thick, twiggy sprawl; saddled or in crotch

WHERE: On branches next to trunk, horizontal fork away from trunk, in a crotch; conifer or hardwood forest, often along edges; suburban and urban areas (especially near acorns, bird feeders, other food)

SHAPE: Base sprawling, cup tighter

BUILDER AND MATERIALS: Both birds break large and small twigs from live branches, assemble them, then add twigs, roots, and sometimes mud. Rootlets line the cup. String, tarp strands, cloth, and birch bark may garnish the exterior.

D: 7–8"   H: 4–4.25"   G: 10–25'

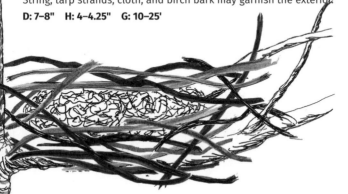

NESTS MADE OF STICKS, MOSTLY 10 INCHES TO 6 FEET DIAMETER

    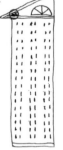

GREAT BLUE HERON

Many nests; near water, fresh or salt; colonial nester

D: 24–48"
H: 30–100+"

Throughout

AMERICAN CROW

Flattish on limb or cone-shaped at trunk in upper ⅓ of tree

D: 12–18"
H: 10–70'

Throughout

BALD EAGLE

One third down from crown

D: 4–6'
H: 40–100'*

OSPREY

Top of tree, pole, or bridge

D: 2.5–6'
H: 10–60'*

RED-TAILED HAWK

In open habitats; often in top of tree; also in cities on skyscrapers

D: 20–36"
H: 35–100'

Throughout

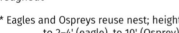

* Eagles and Ospreys reuse nest; height to 2–4' (eagle), to 10' (Osprey).

	D	G	Location	Saucer, platform

A. COLONIAL NESTERS: SEVERAL NESTS PER TREE OR SEVERAL TO MANY NESTS IN AREA

	D	G	Location	Saucer, platform
Night Heron, Black-cr.	12–24"	Ground–40+'	Wetlands, salt or fresh water	Yes
Night Heron, Yellow-cr.*	18–26"	15–75'	Shrub or tree, salt or fresh water	Yes
Egret, Great*		24–36" Ground–40+'	Shrub, top of tree; usually over water	Yes
Egret, Snowy	12–24"	5–10'	Shrub, tree; coastal, Gulf north to S. ME	Yes

*May also nest singly

B. NOT COLONIAL NESTERS **Great Horned Owls** sometimes repurpose hawk and crow nests.

	D	G	Location
Heron, Green	8–15"	10–20+'	Thicket, shrub, tree; near or over water

● **Hawks:** Nests overlap in size, location in tree, habitat; identification can be difficult from below.

	D	G	Location
Broad-winged	10–18"	24–40'	Low in tall tree; deciduous, mixed woods
Red-shouldered	15–28"	20–26'	Below top of tree; deciduous, mixed woods
Cooper's	8–26"	25–50'	~⅓ below top of tree; open habitats

Black-crowned Night-heron · Yellow-crowned Night-heron · Great Egret · Green Heron · Broad-winged Hawk · Red-shouldered Hawk · Cooper's Hawk

NEST IN CAVITY   p. 46–47 only: **D** = DECIDUOUS, **C** = CONIFEROUS
A. EXCAVATES OWN CAVITY IN A TREE (for other choices, see p. 48)

	Pileated Woodpecker	Northern Flicker	Red-bellied Woodpecker	Hairy Woodpecker	Yellow-bellied Sapsucker
Hole	Oval, triangular At base 3.5–4" H: 3.25"	Round D: ~3" [2–4"]	Round D: 2 x 2.25"	Oblong D: 2" H: 2.3"	Round D: 1.25–1.5"
Tree	Usually dead but sound	Dead	Dead or dead limb in live tree	Dead section of live tree	Usually dead deciduous
Habitat	**C**, **D** forests, mixed woodlands	Open **C**, **D** woods; roadsides; woodlots	**C**, **D** forests; suburbs, shade trees, gardens	**C**, **D** forests; wooded wetlands	**C**, **D** mixed forests; woodlots
Reuses?	Rarely	Yes	Not usually	No	Yes
Who uses a drilled or natural cavity with this size hole?	Saw-whet Owl Wood Duck	Saw-whet Owl	Great Crested Flycatcher		—

in. | 1 | 2 | 3 | 4 | 5

Breed throughout:
Downy, Hairy, Flicker

Downy Woodpecker	Red-breasted Nuthatch (p. 49)	Chickadees* Black-capped (p. 54)	Carolina
Round, oval D: 1.25"	Round D: 1–1.5"	Round D: 1.1"	Round D: 1.5"
Usually dead or dying	Dead or rotting	Rotten stub or stump	
Open mixed-growth forest, wetlands	C forest; D woods	C/D forests, open woods	Mixed, D woods, wetlands, suburbs
No	Sometimes	—	—
Bluebird, p. 54; White-breasted Nuthatch, p. 49; Tree Swallow, p. 52; wrens, p. 52–53; titmouse and starling, M p. 51	—	—	—

*May drill a cavity

Pileated Woodpecker

Red-bellied Woodpecker

Yellow-bellied Sapsucker

B. EXCAVATES OWN CAVITY IN SOIL, SAND, OR GRAVEL BANK

	Belted Kingfisher	Bank Swallow
Hole	5" roundish	1.5–3" roundish

C. USUALLY USES CAVITY IN ROOTS OF BLOWDOWN

May also use roots along stream or fill a rock crevice with moss and excavate into it

Winter Wren

D. USES LARGE NATURAL CAVITY

Wood Duck (p. 51)

Belted Kingfisher

Bank Swallow

Winter Wren

WINTER WREN

WHERE: Coniferous and deciduous forests and woodlands

BUILDER AND MATERIALS: Male starts several nests, each of moss, twigs, rootlets, plant stems, and fine grasses. Female chooses one, lining it with fine rootlets, hair, and feathers. Moss and a sprig of conifer are characteristic. (See p. 8 re: unused nests.)

Opening 1"   G: Few–25'

WHITE-BREASTED NUTHATCH

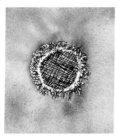

WHERE: More often in deciduous than coniferous forests but can be found in both

BUILDER AND MATERIALS: The pair does not drill but rather uses a natural or small woodpecker cavity. The birds smear the hole rim with a foul-smelling mash of insects, presumably to deter other insects or predators, or to cover the scent of their chicks.

Hole D: 1.25"   G: 15–60'

RED-BREASTED NUTHATCH

WHERE: Dead tree, live tree with rotten wood, standing stump; in either conifer or hardwood (often aspen, which has relatively soft wood); RB hardly ever uses a nest box.

BUILDER AND MATERIALS: Both birds excavate the cavity; the female builds a nest inside. The pair transports pine pitch—mouthful by mouthful—to the rim of the cavity, smearing it along the opening. The parents continue this process until the chicks have fledged.

Hole D: ~1" [–1.5"]   G: 15' [5–40']

NEST IN BOX

Use this key only at the end of the season after birds have left.
Shell fragments, if present, can be useful with identification.

Dots   **Spots**   **Blotches**

A. TWIGS GENERALLY NOT USED IN NEST

			Page

Lining usually feathers

Nest domed	Eggs whitish, greenish with brown or gray dots	**House Sparrow**	51
Nest a cup	Eggs white	**Tree Swallow**	52

Lining may include feathers and:

Plant down, hair	Eggs white with reddish-brown spots	**Chickadee, Black-capped**	54
Plant down, hair	As above, but dots to small blotches	**Chickadee, Carolina**	54

No feathers; lining includes:

Mostly fine grasses	Eggs pale blue, no markings	**Eastern Bluebird**	54
Fine grasses, soft shreds of inner bark, fur, hair	Eggs white with lavender or light-brown spots	**White-breasted Nuthatch**	49
Hair, fur, string	Eggs creamy or white with lavender, purple, or reddish-brown spots	**Tufted Titmouse**	M 51

B. NEST SOMETIMES OR REGULARLY CONTAINS SMALL TWIGS WITH OTHER MATERIALS | Page

Often includes snakeskin or strips of plastic	Eggs yellowish, pinkish with dark brown–purple blotches	**Great Crested Flycatcher**	55
Green leaves as garnish	Eggs white; often uses multibird house	**Purple Martin**	M below
Made with various materials, including trash; green garnish; chick droppings common in nest before chicks fledge		**European Starling**	M below

C. NEST OF TWIGS AND OTHER MATERIALS, USUALLY DOMED WITH SIDE ENTRANCE

Mostly twigs	Eggs white with reddish-brownish dots	**House Wren**	52
More variety in materials	Eggs white-pink with many brown spots	**Carolina Wren**	53

D. NO NESTING MATERIALS ADDED; BOX ~11" SQUARE

Natural cavities and boxes placed along wetland edges	Eggs creamy white or yellowish tan	**Wood Duck**	M below

Purple Martin

Tufted Titmouse

Wood Duck

Throughout:
House Sparrow, European Starling

TREE SWALLOW

Grasses and feathers

WHERE: Nest boxes; natural or woodpecker cavity in open areas (fields near water, wetlands), near humans

BUILDER AND MATERIALS: Female builds a simple nest of dry grasses covered with many feathers.

HOUSE WREN

Sticks and feathers; chicks defecate in the nest.

WHERE: Near buildings in a hole, corner, or crevice in gutter or eves; a bucket, grill, or nest box; in woodpecker or natural cavity along woodland borders; in open woodlands; suburban parks and gardens

SIZE: Sometimes bird fills entire cavity.

BUILDER AND MATERIALS: The male builds rough nests; the female inspects, chooses one, and finishes it—or makes another. The nest is composed mostly of twigs, twiglets, and bark strips dropped into the cavity, with a few grasses or feathers as lining. Wrens will evict bluebirds and other species, then rebuild for themselves.

CAROLINA WREN
Creative cavities

WHERE: Around houses in nest boxes; containers such as flowerpots, pails, or grills; covered nooks and crannies of buildings. In the wild, in natural cavities to 10' aboveground in shrubby woods, thickets, and open land reverting to shrubs and weeds.

SHAPE: Even in a box, the nest is domed with a side entrance.

BUILDER AND MATERIALS: Both birds build, using twigs, bark strips, grasses, leaves, plant stalks, twine, and other materials; they line with moss, fine grasses, and feathers, sometimes including a few pieces of snakeskin or plastic.

| in. | | 1 | | 2 | | 3 | | 4 | | 5 |

EASTERN BLUEBIRD

Shell pieces blue

WHERE: In the wild, cavity or woodpecker hole to 50' in open country or open woods with little understory; along roads in rural areas; near humans

BUILDER AND MATERIALS: The male attracts the female to the cavity or box, then the female builds the nest within using dried grass, plant stems, and often pine needles or tiny twigs. For the lining, she uses fine grasses.

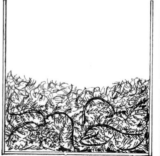

CHICKADEES

BC: Felted lining

WHERE: For a tree cavity, the pair chooses a rotten stub or stump in mixed, deciduous, or open woods. The holes are 4–8' (Black-capped) and 2–25' (Carolina) aboveground.

BUILDER AND MATERIALS: Female uses moss and other materials for the base, then lines with hair and plant down (BC) or plant fiber (CC) and other soft materials.

BC

CC

GREAT CRESTED FLYCATCHER

Larger hole for larger bird; snakeskin

WHERE: Natural or woodpecker cavity in open woodlands (especially second growth), trees bordering clearings, roads; near ground to 70' high

BUILDER AND MATERIALS: Chiefly female, stuffing twigs, grass, stems, and any of these materials: rootlets, pine needles, feathers, fur, human hair, cloth, string, shells, moss, paper, shed snakeskin (deters predators?), or plastic (resembles snakeskin?). The female builds a cup amid the debris.

Nest box entrance

D: 2–2.3"

Inner cup D: 3–3.5"

Inner depth: 1.5–2"

NEST ON/IN BUILDING, CHIMNEY, BRIDGE, OR OTHER STRUCTURES   **Page**

Makes no nest	Lays eggs on barn beam (**Barn Owl**), flat roof (**Common Nighthawk**)		—
Inside building	Cup on rafter or half cup against wall	**Barn Swallow**	58

Outside building   Under an eve, below a porch or shed roof, in a nook or crevice

- Gourd-shaped mud nest with side entrance, against wall   **Cliff Swallow**   59
- Thin platform of sticks in gutter, under eve, similar sites   **Mourning Dove**   41
- Domed with side entrance, in eves, crevices, or anything with cover
  - Lining grasses, rootlets, etc., with some feathers   **Carolina Wren, House Wren**   52–53
  - Lining usually entirely feathers   **House Sparrow**   M 51
- Cup on horizontal surface (Eastern Phoebe may also nest on wall)
  - Pillbox with exterior of grasses   **American Robin**   34
  - Cup with exterior of moss   **Eastern Phoebe**   57
- Nests in a colony in nooks, crannies, birdhouse   **Purple Martin**   M 51

Outside on roof or in crannies of skyscraper		**Red-tailed Hawk**	44–45
Chimney	On inside wall, **Chimney Swift** (right) On top of, **Osprey**, p. 44		
Bridge	On, **Cliff Swallow**, p. 59; **Osprey**, p. 44 Underside of, **Barn Swallow**, p. 58; **Eastern Phoebe**, p. 57		

Chimney Swift: Nest is a crescent of sticks held together by saliva.

EASTERN PHOEBE

D: 4–4.5" with base to ~8+"
H: 2" over time increasing to 4"

WHERE: Under eave, bridge, high deck; on rafter or beam; in the wild, in steep, rocky, protected area (saddled, to 15')

SHAPE: Cup; from below may look like a mound of moss; phoebes reuse nests, which become bigger over time

BUILDER AND MATERIALS: Female mixes mud, plant stems, and moss for base. She lines with fine grasses, fibers, hair, and pine needles, then covers the outside with moss; mud may show through.

in.   1   2   3   4   5

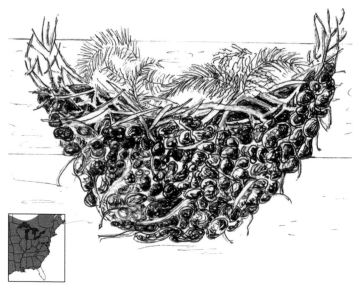

BARN SWALLOW

Pairs nest singly or sometimes within a loose colony.

WHERE: Under bridges, inside barns and out-buildings

BUILDER AND MATERIALS: Both birds build, carrying—in their throats and mouths—gobs of mud mixed with grass. They line with feathers and grasses. If the previous nest is relatively free from parasites, they may simply replace the feathers and reinforce the rim.

On wall, D: 5" wide   Flat on beam, D: ~5"

| in. | | 1 | | 2 | | 3 | | 4 | | 5 |

CLIFF SWALLOW

Within range, nesting may be sparse, localized.

WHERE: On buildings, bridges, or similar structures, usually where a vertical surface abuts a horizontal surface, providing protection; often near water (mud, insects)

SHAPE: Gourd or bottle

BUILDER AND MATERIALS: Both male and female create with mud and grass, then line with small amount of grass, feathers.

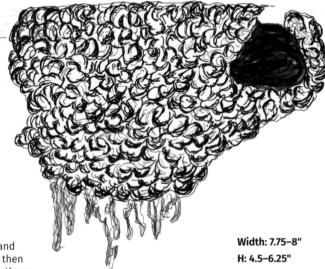

Width: 7.75–8"

H: 4.5–6.25"

Hole D: 1.75 x 2"

NOT BIRD NESTS

SQUIRREL

A squirrel nest, called a drey, is a messy, roundish mass of twigs, bark, and/or leaves, with grass lining the interior. The drey can be next to the trunk or out on a limb.

Flying, D: 8"

Red, D: 10–12"

Gray and Fox, D: 12–20"

G: 30–45'

MOUSE

Deer and white-footed mice often use abandoned bird nests to cache berries, nuts, and other food. Sometimes they cover the nest with grasses, make a side entrance, and line with plant down—making a look-alike, domed wren nest (wrens, in contrast, build in cavities or enclosures). Some mice in the genus *Peromyscus* carry bacteria in their gut that triggers over-compensation. Instead of building a snug little nest, they build a snug huge nest, mounding layers of grasses on and around the abandoned bird nest.

D: From 4.5" (normal mouse) to 6–8+" (affected mouse)

G: ~5–20' [–80']   Side hole: 0.5–0.75"

ACKNOWLEDGMENTS: Thank you all. **To Ben, who got us there and back again.** Bernd Heinrich (Professor Emeritus of Biology, University of Vermont) and Jerome Longcore (retired, U.S. Geological Service), who helped me identify problematic nests and shared key details; Maine Master Naturalist graduates, who tested many early keys; byron murray, his colleagues, and students at Guelph Outdoor School, who field-tested this book; Beth Brooke, Clare Cole, Michaeline Mulvey, Cheryl Ring, and Tina Wood, who helped in so many ways; and Jeremiah Trimble and Kate Eldridge, who arranged access to the amazing nest collection at Harvard University's Museum of Comparative Zoology. Any errors are, of course, my own.

Other books in the pocket-size *Finder* series:

FOR US AND CANADA EAST OF THE ROCKIES

Berry Finder native plants with fleshy fruits

Bird Finder frequently seen birds

Fern Finder native ferns of the Midwest and Northeast

Flower Finder spring wildflowers and flower families

Life on Intertidal Rocks organisms of the North Atlantic Coast

Scat Finder mammal scat

Track Finder mammal tracks and footprints

Tree Finder native and common introduced trees

Winter Tree Finder leafless winter trees

Winter Weed Finder dry plants in winter

FOR STARGAZERS

Constellation Finder patterns in the night sky and star stories

FOR FORAGERS

Mushroom Finder fungi of North America

Dorcas S. Miller, founding president of the Maine Master Naturalist Program, has written more than a dozen books, including *Track Finder, Scat Finder, Winter Weed Finder, Berry Finder*, and *Constellation Finder*. Her *Finder* books have sold more than half a million copies.

NATURE STUDY GUIDES are published by AdventureKEEN, 2204 1st Ave. S., Suite 102, Birmingham, AL 35233; 800-678-7006; naturestudy.com. See shop.adventurewithkeen.com for our full line of nature and outdoor activity guides by ADVENTURE PUBLICATIONS, MENASHA RIDGE PRESS, and WILDERNESS PRESS, including many guides for birding, wildflowers, rocks, and trees, plus regional and national parks, hiking, camping, backpacking, and more.